Around the Sun Without a Sail

Around the Sun Without a Sail

Poems

Richard Fenwick

Plaid Condor Press • 2012

Copyright © 2012 by Richard Fenwick

All rights reserved. Except for brief quotations in critical articles or reviews, no part of this book may be reproduced in any manner without the author's prior written approval.

Published 2012 by Plaid Condor Press

The text of this book is set in Palatino Linotype

Second Edition

ISBN: 978-0-61566-055-4

For Marlene Rose Sloss
1939 – 2011

…If you were here,
I'd pluck this trembling globe to show
how beautiful a thing can be
a breath will tear away.

A Dandelion for My Mother
Jean Nordhaus

contents

Poets of a Dead Language   3

one

Halfway Point   7
One Moment   8
Helsinki   10
Winter Rye   12
The Barren Bits   13
In Praise of Profanity   15
Coffee Shop Noise   16
A Short Walk on the Shimokita Peninsula   18
Birthday Song   20

two

And Then the Lighting of the Lamps   23
Settling Down   24
To the Twenty-Something Girl Who Winked   26
The Tin Chair   27
River of Faces   28
Watermelon   30
Council House   31
A Minor Ode to Poetry   33
Geography   34

three

Autopsis   37

four

Burning Matches   43
Hiroshima   45
Barents Sea Monastery   47
Topeka   48
Fourth of July   50
Before a Cold Front Can Emerge   52
Postcard from Russia   54
Liliya   55

five

Four O'clock Poem   59
From My Mother's Eyes   60
Pushkin on Twitter   62
Andromeda   63
Standing Still with Monet   64
Back in the Day   66
Symmetry   68
Hirosaki Castle   70

Around the Sun Without a Sail   73

Notes   75
Acknowledgments   77
About the Author   79

Around the Sun Without a Sail

Poets of a Dead Language

> *Place, man, cattle, creature-kind,*
> *& tree of every image*
> *taking place.*
>
> – Akhenaton, 3,400 years ago

Let's imagine them in a circle
at a fire pit that has burned for days,
and final feathers of sun to paint
the sky in every shade of red.

Perhaps they sip a sour wine
as the quiet one chants a tribal tale:
dragon smoke and gathered clouds
black, like nighttime rivers,

or how the moon scrubs demons
to guard them as they sleep.
Let's say they had a word for him
and render it as *poet*. Let's say

we sip our wine and speak
his tongue, draped in a thousand
winters past, chant our tales
beside this gray-scaled fire,

each word a stone that rings
our pit in songs of songs, each
memory a dead poet, tossed
like bone-white paper planes
in twilight skeins of time.

one

At rest, however, in the middle of everything is the sun

Nicolas Copernicus

Halfway Point

She dips an oar from an ash canoe
into the lake's dark surface,
pulls herself toward its center
to push away the past, or
future, or even tonight's moon.

A fish leaps, concentric circles,
two small branches drift to shore
as her oar cuts deep into the skin
of water, the lake's thin flesh.

Resting it against her thighs,
she glides until each ripple fades,
and wonders if she should return
to their small white dock

or complete the lonely journey
to the cottage on the other side.

One Moment

For just one moment
everything in the room makes sense:
the mahogany guitar upright
and perched on its steel pedestal,
all the novels on undusted shelves,
even the cat curled at my leg
purring in her softest key.

It's a moment I can admire
with a song of incoming e-mail,
a red coffee cup spilling steam
into the cool air of this house,

the way it tumbles end-
over-end to disappear behind
a chair, to reappear
with every drop of water singing
against last night's dinner plates.

I wonder if astronauts, whirling
through space, have known
this moment, or timeworn
scientists – prior to discovery –
managed first to admire quills
dipped into wet, India ink.

And though I'm late and must
take trash to street, shave
and shower, clip and groom,
this moment – as opposed
to all the others – was a pleasure,

with its wintry shadows cast
against a mirror hanging
by my window, where just now
a red-throated hummingbird
hovered and sped away,

as I should, once I've stored
this moment in the warehouse
of my mind, placing it
beside the memories of you
slipping softly in the room.

Helsinki

My small black journal
would have borne a hundred poems –
or at least a thousand lies –
had I not forgotten it in Helsinki

where I sat in a hotel bar
watching from my poet's window
as city workers in white overalls
swept up piles of clean snow,

firemen threw candied tarts
at packs of children whose hands
rose like exclamation marks
to a sky full of birds and blue.

I only wish I could remember
the poems hidden in that book:
a piece about my mother's smile,
the comparison I once made
between Freud and Seattle,

the bartender in his red
waistcoat, selecting my vodka,
saying *you will drink Finnish*,
how crisp and bare the trees were
on the Esplandi, pale-haired
women waving back at me.

These were American poems,
casual observations from airports,
cafés, places you would find
in San Antonio or Traverse City,

perhaps a tiny bistro, beachside
near Delray, all the places
I carried the journal, as if
it was a part of me,

though Helsinki – a city I loved –
decided to swallow its leather
whole, as I sipped too much vodka
in a true display of Finnish force.

Winter Rye
For JNF

On an evening of poetry,
my mind drifts back to May
when the pale-green Bermuda
replaced the Winter Rye.
We closed her niche like
a midnight whisper across
a wide expanse of bed,
and gathered at my father's
house, where he tended
to every guest, reverential,
pouring wine, smiling
at nervous jokes to console us –
the way a poem does – when
rain pushed us indoors.
Now spring is gone, summer
has leaked in, the Bermuda
is full and faint. Yet
I think of him in May,
graceful with the wine, stylish
in a coat and tie, peaceful
as he stood so still
in the last small patch
of dark-green Winter Rye.

The Barren Bits

From the passenger's seat
of your car, I'm inside a journal
writing of the barren bits
between Phoenix and L.A.,

how we're running from
a wren atop a barrel cactus,
or swift vans filled with children
near enough now to Blythe,
a truck missing a left rear tire.

As I write, you interrupt me
to say you wish we were
running to Carolina, and my pen
wanders past the mesquite
and palo verde trees

to sycamores and elms, wild grass
growing green upon a creek bed,
a small mountain cabin
with a curl of smoke lifting
from its red brick stack.

There's a swing on the porch,
a good guitar lying near
the front window, and inside
I can even see a bottle of wine
in a bucket of melting ice,
and hear your voice calling

from a back bedroom, asking me
to put away the journal,
to close the door once the dog
has slipped out, to fill our glasses

before I pad the wood floor,
like a buck in overgrown woods,
to raise a shade and cast sunlight
across your favorite print,

that exceptional red poppy
painted for us by O'Keeffe.

In Praise of Profanity

Yellow chrysanthemums
light this overly drab kitchen
where she cooks hash browns,
the sweet scent of sausage
reminding me of another house,
a grandfather's kitchen
near Sault Ste. Marie,
pine needles in thick woods,
lichens on rocks,
baskets of blueberries for pies.
There was sweet corn at night,
Great Northern Pike
and baked potatoes piled
with sour cream, and here
she cooks for me, browning
butter to scramble eggs
as I sit at our table
reading old passages from
a notebook, where I've written –
inexplicably – that love
is a four-letter word.

Coffee Shop Noise

In a rare burst of November sun,
I sat outside a coffee shop
watching for signs of poetry,

listening to white noise filter
across the sidewalk, stacking notes
in a journal that trickled
from blue pen to yellow page.

I wrote of a white-button moon
lying flat on the sky's blue shirt,
telephone wires stretched high

like lines on sheet music, birds
perched on them as quarter notes
over idling or sleeping cars.

I jotted small poems dedicated
to the couple arguing a wedding,
flicking angry cigarettes at
a plastic ashtray, black lab
panting at their feet,

and to the woman behind me
growling for sugar, her husband's
metal chair scraping concrete
as he jumped to rescue her,

and of course I wrote a poem
dedicated to you,
sitting at your corner table
under a weathered poster
of Sri Lanka, stacking notes
in your tiny book,

and how I wondered if
you were writing about me,
the gray-haired man whose table
had just been covered in shade.

A Short Walk on the Shimokita Peninsula

If you're reading this,
please note I've added a sunset filled
with pink and orange popcorn clouds
in a swimming pool sky, stringy
contrails of passing planes, a breeze
to whisper in your ears.

Let me throw in a willow tree
as it tastes the water of a small trout brook,
the steady patter making you weary
too early in the day.

Since we've come this far,
why don't we add a sonnet by Shakespeare,
one he's asked us to revise for him
given our flair for poetry.

Now imagine: none of this exists,
no sky filled with clouds, no trees sipping
from a creek, and Shakespeare
doesn't need our help
to write one of a thousand sonnets.

What there is, dear reader,
is a sliver of moon smiling down
through the last turquoise of this day
while we march our wooded trail,

my arm around your shoulder
watching the earth move and kissing it –
like a kite kisses the sky –
on both of its beautiful, blue cheeks.

Birthday Song

We were eating Red Snapper
when she poured a glass of wine,
candles dancing like Salomé
and the seven veils,

to talk of what little we knew
about Puccini and operas, arias,
watching our shadows tremble
on the opposite wall.

I proposed a small toast to
the inadequate mysteries of youth,
as she glanced at me across
the table, and smiled through

the candles to ring her glass
against mine, the music of wine
filling the nook like bells
at Saint Anthony's. And after

I dried wet dishes, I took her
in my arms to hum some
Buddy Holly tune, and danced
her down a half-lit hall,

our shadows finally merging.
Our shadows always merging.

two

The solar system has no anxiety about its reputation

Ralph Waldo Emerson

And Then the Lighting of the Lamps

Weathered by too much sun
    she sweeps her life's cobwebs
        under a vanity heavy with books.
            She doesn't want to answer
              when he calls –
        turns instead to say she's sorry,
    that it will all work out once
    someone turns on the battered lamp
in the darkest corner of the room.

Settling Down
For CY

Had I thought of it years ago,
I would have told you
how my heart was a jackhammer
that night in your father's car,
though we were more like boxcars

coupling, the racket of tooth
against tooth, a hint of blood,
a desperate desire to freeze time
as seconds became days,
each hour a span of light years.

I would have said your dark hair
reminded me of falling water,
your canted eyes of secrets –
or an ancient Asian wisdom
you wanted to address –

and how much I desired
the moment to linger, like fog
on a day that begs for sun.

Of course I didn't say this,
and boys become men,
years pass like lightning strikes
in harvested fields, rainbows lead
to houses tucked into ends
of cul-de-sacs. And yet

I have to say, if it happens
to be October, and the moon
is full and fat with a breeze
rising from the wet night grass,
my thoughts of you become
the wooden bridge that spans

my mainland to the island
of memories I've saved,
and when that occurs I close
my eyes to think of you holding
tight to my waist,

or to a grandchild whose smile
reveals a tooth or two,
and close this book, the one
I began two days ago

of the young man
running wild through Kristiania,
who can't quite decide
the significance of his hunger.

To the Twenty-Something Girl Who Winked

It's not that I don't admire
the reds and greens running down
both arms and across your thighs,

it's just that I'd be despondent
next to all that ink, knowing
I could never quite undress you.

The Tin Chair

She kept the old lawn chair,
shaped like an open-faced clam
and rusted red from rain,
in a corner of the garage
by a crumpled box of books.

She tried to clean it once,
though bits of him fell from
its surfaces like snow:

silver grips where he held
his hands, flecks of paint –
the color of flamingoes –
poking through the rust,

how the chair exhaled as
she pressed into its skeleton.

Now, when a mask of hail
covers the grass, she curls
inside the tin chair's seat,
reaching her hands
to the ceiling where he

once penciled a promise
of paint, to feel the earth
adjust itself beneath her.

River of Faces
   For Jake Mercer

In summer, Granddad's mules
ground at bits and complained
along their length of reins
as he cursed the sun, one hand
raised to eyes as weathered
as a whip, coaxing the team
across Kentucky bottom-lands.
Later, with lather spread
across their necks, or dripping
to their hooves, he poured
the mules and himself, like
oil to water, into the shade
of a grass-lined levee, where
they rested by the river.

My father and I stood alone
left of center at the Vietnam
Memorial Wall. I thought of him
laughing as he told me
of mortar attacks at Pleiku base,
night skies flared with fire
peppering the fence, mornings
of black-clad men draped
across it like wet laundry
on a barbed-wire clothesline.

Sometimes he cried, tears
staining the air between us,
his fists filled with the metal darts
he once packed inside
thousand-pound bombs
that cut away sweet mango trees,
fields of rice, and sampans
on rivers brimmed with rain,
rivers without levees
casting a shade to rest in
when the seasons soured.

There: He raised his hand
to lay it flat on coal-black
stone to stroke the face
of *Jacob E. Mercer*,
and as I tried to coax him
to the shadows, he slipped
into the stream, like oil
to water, and swam along
the granite wall, each face
whispering out
that river's rightful name.

Watermelon

Let me slice open a watermelon
to watch the juice slip down the tip
of my knife and onto the plate.

With a tablespoon, I'll cut divots
and press them with my tongue
against the roof of my mouth

as the icy pulp crumbles away,
leaving nothing but a sweetness
and black and white seeds

piled in a green-glass bowl,
as I spoon the rest down
to the outer rind, each bite cool
against my teeth, the juices

exploding in my mouth
like watermelon does,
and running down my chin
like watermelon will.

Council House

Valentina sits alone
in the shade of palo verde trees,
dingy white wicker on grass
near the center of town.

Beside her lies a crossword,
her Cyrillic letters exact: across,
now down, like ghetto streets
in old Odessa.

I take her hand to say hello,
and feel the tattered scar
of an old barbed-wire wound,
watch her toothless smile
moving: *dobriy dyen*, she says.

Ten years ago she left,
by then infirm, to join a son
who wrote and said: *Mama,
we have synagogues.*

There were few prayers in Ukraine.

Through Venice to New York
they pushed her, as she does now
a red and black walker, colors
of armbands in devil's ink.

And she has explained to me
the camps, the kilometers walked,
the common graves they dug
for firing squads to fill,
how hunger hollows the mind,

or what passes through it
when an orchestra plays
a tango of death. She whispers
it in Russian: *tango smerti*.

Fingering her scar like
she might a stream of tears,
she pulls down her sleeve to say

she didn't mind leaving
at such an age, but I see her
scan the desert sky, as a flock

of military jets pass over,
and two bold clouds wash
the deep blue stain, like
a blanket of withering snow.

A Minor Ode to Poetry

If I were to try to explain
why I take up time with poetry,
I would tell you, of course,
about the black tea kettle
you've left on a back burner,

or this glass of icy water
sweating on a tatted coaster.
I'd be compelled to say
green leaves turn blood red
in autumn, winters are

a kind of death, springs rebirth,
summers just the hot group
of months between the two.

And if you ask if bees
in orange blossoms, sparrows
in bird baths, or the cat chirping
at them from a window
are all parts of my poetry,

I will nod my head, take up
a number two pencil, and write
a first draft to remind you –
because I always want
to remind you – that love
is like a red, red rose.

Geography

In anticipation of my birthday,
I've decided not to scratch my head
searching for perfect nouns, verbs
to fill an empty space on a page.
I won't worry about modifiers
or similes that refuse to settle in,
or the scolded child of passive voice.
No, today I will sit to admire
the prints on this wall, the map
posted over my cluttered desk
with its question mark of Africa,
its blue seahorse of Japan,
the stingray and its tail made
from the Aleutians and Alaska.
This is where I'll wait
for my birth hour, which arrives
each year like summer gossip,
with promises of ten more winters
and an abundance of more gray hair.
I will leave it all behind
to read Whitman or Paz, perhaps
a bit of George Bilgere,
and after I have a sandwich
with a Dutch or Belgian beer,
I'll return alone to my map
where my mouth begins to water
as I taste the bone-in ribeye
that is always South America.

three

*It is a loss, both to himself and others,
when a traveler does not observe*

"Hints to Travelers", the Royal Geographical Society

Autopsis

> For my mother

I.

In the geography of this world, I am barefoot in sand
    with a cup of tea steeped in ritual ways, mixed

with cream that swirls amid the rich herbs to form
    a favorite shade, an earthy tone of lean clay.

This morning's wind trusses beach to ocean, ocean
    to globe, globe to the tattered path we spin upon.

Still, today tides rise, crabs skittle across the beach,
    a white mass floats in the sky that is not a moon

or a school of flying fish, but a flock of gulls that hovers
    near a fisher's fantail, beyond the waves

as equal to this morning as my tea. The surf blends
    with sun, the horizon is gray, the angels perch like

pelicans on the rotted wood of docks. This morning,
    the world is as hopeless as a poem.

II.

I have been to Lake Ladoga
near the Baltic Sea, where a fisherman
led me to his bucket of silvery smelt,
their pneumatic gills gasping
like piston engines in pinkish oil.

When beggar gypsies jumped upon
a subway train, I turned to read
the city maps, to sip more tea, to watch
the hooded *babushkas* inspect their
darkly rolled umbrellas.

Digression: Once, as we drank whiskey on a rooftop in Baltimore, I found myself counting stars that floated like packs of burnt balloons. That night, the sky spoke from between two clouds: *there are only moments,* it said, before bowing to whiskey and winter.

The Atlantic is still dark,
it burdens itself and moves,
and soon will turn plum-purple.

The gulls hover at the fantail,
as a crewman pitches baitfish
into the struggling sky,
and still they cry for more.

III.

Sometimes, a poem of lilies
streaked in gold and thriving
in a blue vase can be
a simple poem of lilies
streaked in gold and thriving.

When I was four, leaves fell
mid-air between branch and earth,
as did I, from the branch,
afraid to let go, to fall.

My mother came and said:
open wide your eyes and palms.

Sometimes, a poem of lilies
streaked in gold and thriving
in a blue vase can be
a prescription for grace.

I see the tired beach and fear
the fall. I think I may forget
to open wide my eyes and palms,

afraid of angels perched
on rotted logs, silvery smelt
sucking air, even the lilies
she bought in Amsterdam
when I was a boy.

The waves that round me
are open eyes and palms,
coastal beacons begging ships
to clear the craggy shore,

and when it's time, I want
to let go into the crèche of leaves
below, to open wide
my eyes and palms. I want

to remember the prescription.

Sometimes, a poem of lilies
streaked in gold and thriving
in a blue vase is as graceful
as a mother's quiet smile,

and as a last light dances
across the Atlantic's dark face,
the sun narrows to its
final filament, faint and full.

Open wide your eyes and palms.

When it's time,
I want to fall with the weight
of lilies, streaked in grace,

wide-eyed and thriving.

four

> *Мечты, мечты! где ваша сладость?*
> *(Dreams, dreams! Where is your sweetness?)*
>
> Alexander Pushkin

Burning Matches

Vladimir rocks near a window
in his mother's chair,
and sings Ukrainian lullabies
to the room, as two black flies orbit
like warplanes near Odessa,

where he and his brother
were thrown like pigs to pens,
two small boys with rheumy eyes,
two Jews struck, used, thrown
like matches to the ground
to sizzle in a brackish mud.

Their mother crawled beneath
wire and bribed a guard whose leer
was a form of forgiveness
when he finished, and begged him
for the boys, though he
offered one, a *Sophie's Choice*,
one boy to take back to a ghetto
of the dead and dying.

Yesterday I visited Vladimir,
winced with him at a toothache
and stuttered in broken Russian
with a man who pretends he's well,
though I see it in his eyes:

how he strikes each match,
squints to watch it burn
and drops it to a bowl – black
like a sarcophagus –
piled high with all the others.

Hiroshima

It's Monday morning, August sixth,
   the heat rises in an air stained
      with imperceptions, the city moves:
         children learn their Kanji symbols,

Shinto priests ring temple bells,
   soldiers call cadence for calisthenics,
      women search for fish and rice
         to cook an evening meal.

There's an indecisive breeze
   that will soon wound the earth,
      as overhead a single bomber plods
         inside the immense sky, droning

like Tibetan monks in prayer,
   headed for downtown Hiroshima.
      The blast flashes, hot as the sun,
         to incinerate everything for a mile,

birds burst apart mid-flight,
   human shadows burn into walls
      that withstand the shock. In two days,
         a poison will erode them, the sick

and blinded begging for water
   before their eyes roll white,
      as ordered chaos crumbles the city
         into a fine, pale ash, though now,

high above, the bomber crew
 watches with curious fascination
  as a cauliflower head of cloud
   rises from the surface, punctures

the stillness of this peaceful day,
 and Hiroshima burns for miles,
  its survivors honoring victims
   within the whispering bamboos.

Barents Sea Monastery

The island's rowboat rots
sliver-by-sliver, half-in and -out
of a sea that strikes the shore
in monotonous, minor tones,

where the sky has been gray so long,
years ago they quit searching.

Gull cries and dirges, flowers
emerge as a sign, hidden
by a northern sea that has
had its way with everything,

and still, when rabid gasps
of wind lash them, they grip
their tattered bibles, icons
of the virgin mother,
and whisper in a desolate air:

О Господи! я не достоин!
(Oh Lord! I am not worthy!)

Topeka

For Sara and T.A.

In what I call my writing room,
a light rain whispers at the window
as though the desert knows to cry
in August. I'm thinking of Topeka –

twenty-ninth street and cutoff jeans –
BBs fired into bushes manned
by hissing cousins, their snake noise
turned to yelps beside the creek.

Winters, we walked thin ice
near the spillway by the slough, but
by spring we were sailing
model ships laced with sterno

and firecrackers. We watched them
explode, or melt, at the opposite shore
near a willow, or float in tatters
to where Burnett's mound emptied.

Still, the heaviness of Sunday came,
settled on us at the cemetery near
a sycamore's shade, where my aunt
and uncle rested under the grass.

Gently, we plucked at weeds
spread across them like quilts,
or brought our shears to clip

around the lengthy stone,
its rust-red message hanging
hot in the air, like a sullen whisper
in the apse of a church.

But when small airplanes
sputtered past, we watched the sky
as if we knew the secrets
they made that August day,

when the world tipped
in trap-door clouds,
a deadly breeze at the shore
of a Kansas lake whose name
became an accusation,

where Sara and T.A. bowed
and smiled at each other,
leaning their heads together
for one last and beautiful kiss.

Fourth of July

On the fourth of July,
the men gather by the grill
to watch a cousin burn the dogs,
sipping beer that sweats
in heat that permeates the air,

while the children bellow
through sprinkler heads,
and bees buzz at soda cans,
and dogs huddle on the tile
of the cool kitchen floor.

I eat potato salad and watch
as twilight rubs against us,
the kids still in their cutoffs
chasing fireflies that wink
like distant lighthouses,

and wait for nine o'clock,
when someone issues sparklers
that sizzle like bacon
and arc on a moonless night
that reeks of smoke and match,

as I consider my own boyhood,
how we spit seeds and strummed
chords on box guitars, how
we plugged our ears as uncles
fired roman candles,

or the time a cousin caught hell
for tossing two *Black Cat* firecrackers
toward a shrieking aunt.

But mostly I recall the men
huddled in conspiracy,
their stories laced with words
our mothers never liked,
learning what it meant to say:

now that's a fuckin' fire.

Before a Cold Front Can Emerge

He has asked for rain, which comes
as a sigh, heavy with sorrow
and washes the oak of its leaves
as he files through the photographs.

His father is the first book: black
& white in olive drab, Pall Malls
clamped between teeth, an arm
around a boy, two names etched
against a dark stone wall now.

The second is his son, digital tans,
suede boots and tees,
the obligated smiles and eyes,
an arm around another boy.

High up, a third book stands
like a headstone in a weedy field:
the book of funerals, dusted
in begrudging ways, hauled out
when someone calls for snow.

But this is Saturday, and he has
leaves to rake, chores to do
before a cold front can emerge,
when fall departs the hemisphere,

and as bullets of rain dance
against the windows,
he senses the oak's slick roots
refusing to grip the earth

that is circled by a moon
as it circles our small sun,
and a son around a father, all
in their odd and elegant ways.

Postcard from Russia

For fifteen minutes
I've been reading in Russian
to a woman who knows nothing
of the language. She says
she loves Tolstoy, Dostoyevsky
frightens her. She doesn't know
I've been reading Balzac.
Soon, I will smile and rub
my hands together – all wicked
and ready – to tell her
everything will work out,
if she'll only let me unravel
a love poem by Pushkin.

Liliya

With gazelle's eyes, she feasted
on Serengeti grass, hovered
like a *Babushka* over pots of potatoes
as her husband explained how

Trotsky was a *Bronshtein*, Lenin
an *Ulyanov*, Stalin – man
of steel – was first a *Dzhugashvili*.

Once a Rostov doctor, she treated
tuberculosis and was proud
of her father, another doctor
purged in the 50s for being a Jew.

I can see her at Pioneer camp:
a young girl skipping rope,
the Azov Sea draped in green
behind her, running as
planes dove in to strafe.

This morning, I watched men
lower her casket to ground
as women scarved in frowns
poured three scoops of earth
across her open heart.

One asked: *is it your first funeral?*
and before I could answer
handed me a bent-over shovel.

I saw the Serengeti then: great cats
rolled across it like stones at river's edge,
the sun fired the sky, daylight
cracked its whip against caked mud,

and a single gazelle feasted
on grass near Baobab trees, as the stars
hid, waiting for night to emerge.

five

> *Here comes the sun (and I say), it's alright*
> George Harrison

Four O'clock Poem

Imagine the furor
if I stepped out naked
and unafraid
into our covered world.
I'd need socks, of course,
the sporty sorts
that cut at the ankles,
though you probably
wouldn't notice,
what with me in the nude,
my birthday suit,
the buff,
like a model in repose
at a night school art class.
Or better yet:
a walrus at Seal Beach
bouncing along the sand
on its way to the foam
of an all-torrential sea.

From My Mother's Eyes

She buried nickels and dimes
into the folds of cakes, and taste
means nothing to a boy
when he's panning for gold.

I claim to be a good father
because of her yielding hands,
the thin smiles when she swept
colored shards of a vase
shattered by an errant ball.

I'd like to say she taught me
the art of an embrace
amid rivulets of tears that sucked
oxygen from every room,

or the skill of folding tissues
to use, again and again,
on noses too new to breathe in
the simple scent of danger.

But on this rainy Saturday,
as my son marches in
door-to-couch in muddy shoes,
each step painting carpets

like those odd footprints
in an Arthur Murray dance studio,
it takes nearly everything I have –
even as the mud begins to dry –

to wonder what she would have done
to this beautiful, little man,
who doesn't seem to understand
all the choices I actually have.

Pushkin on Twitter

I was three parts Russian @poet
one part Moor, my great-grandfather
an #African gift to @PeterTheGreat.
I wrote sonnets for @Onegin,
small poems for lovers, and @Godunov
would not have lived without me.
The #Decembrists – hung for treason –
loved my *Ode to Freedom*,
though the @Tsar banished me
to #Odessa for it. I was killed
in a #duel at Black Creek, north
of Saint #Petersburg,
and isn't it lovely my last words
were spoken to my library – not
in #French, but mother #Russian:
goodbye, my dear @friends!

Andromeda

This photograph
of Andromeda is a spiral
of water, draining
from your bath,
and I have read how
it dances with us
on the ballroom floor
of space.
Two galaxies spin
and peel away
like onion skins, they
merge as errant stars
that meld within
a galactic storm of fire.
We are galaxies, too,
we dance and peel
our skins
across the universe
of space between us.
Our stars burn
and collide in
a sensuous physics.
Today, there's space;
tonight we flesh out
the elements of time
that can't exist:
dancing in gravity,
colliding in space.

Standing Still with Monet

There's a way we rambled
through the museum, like strangers
separated by paintings
mindful of each other's space.

She blazed ahead as I admired
Monet's villa, its blue sky
washed in clouds above a garden,
dabbed in sinuous strokes.

Monet and I stood on the knoll,
marigolds and hydrangeas
alive in a breeze, as he taught me
impressionism, and how he

painted the light, while the sun
plodded our sky and shadows
grew long toward the villa,

where soon Signor Moreno
would offer us decanted wine,
and Monet would eye the glass
with the intentions of a child,

and as he was about to sing,
she crept up on us to say Gauguin
was two rooms to the left,

though for the day I stood
in a garden at Villa Moreno,
painting the light, and the sun
with its ridiculous, milky smile.

Back in the Day

As I explained long-play albums
to my son, he shook his head
and mumbled *back in the day,
back in the day.*

Patient like a swami, I told him
how the wheel-round disks
were Mayan calendars,
or glossy nights, each groove
a ditch of silence between
solid walls of sound.

I talked about dust jackets
and liner notes, the gentle rub
of felt upon acrylic, how the holes
reminded me of hurricane eyes,
storms with names like
John, Paul, George and Ringo.

He smiled and I continued:
how the swing arm dropped
each album to the platen, how
the needle dipped to meet
its spinning cousin,

and scratches threatened bars
while he shook his head
and whispered: *back in the day,
back in the day.*

Consider my comfort, then,
knowing he'll have children
who will spy his Compact Discs
and whisper: *back in the day,
back in the day,*

and how he'll be compelled
to explain how the light
bounces from a plastic plate
that circles like an album, or
like we do around each other,

or maybe like a turkey vulture,
waiting for his parents to expire.

Symmetry

When my father went to Vietnam,
mom put peonies in her hair
and drove us home to Ontario,
our ragtop Buick Wildcat singing
songs upon the winter roads.

There's a photograph of her
in a long green coat, elegant
and slim, hands clasped at her
head on a cold shore
north of Lake Superior.

In her final days, her hissing
oxygen was, to me, the noise
of cold-soaked cars on turnpikes,
winterized and wheezing
over wet and graying snow,

and I would watch and ask
if I could do anything: fry eggs
with bacon, wash her hair
or take her for a manicure,

though her only request
was that I throw away a black
banana planned for pudding.

There is no symmetry between
then and now, nothing
but a few memories: the Buick
belching smoke and all the songs
she played upon its horn.

But I choose the winter one
of her spinning me
to an Irish song, kneeling
to grasp my shoulders,
a young mother and her son,

laughing, dancing, laughing.

Hirosaki Castle

We stood in the shade
of a cherry tree,
its pink blossoms
as delicate as tissues,
with the ancient castle's
turrets curled
like houses of cards
behind us.
She was a teenager
with black diamond eyes
and a hand to cover
a smile, the other to flash
the peace sign, the *V*
for victory, waiting
for her mother to take
the photograph
of her and the *geijin* –
the foreigner –
in green suede against
a fully gray sky.

Her mother's smile
was an ocean, her words
were the few I knew
in Japanese: *domo arigato
gozaimasu*, thank you,
she said, tilting her head
like it was a question.
And as a cherry blossom
fell near our feet,
the three of us smiled
like caged finches,
nuzzling and waiting for
springtime snow to fall.

Around the Sun Without a Sail

It's time now to put away the words,
the nonsensical phrases I wrote
in the back room of this house.

It's time for the cat to stop sleeping
through my snappy recitations,
as if she'd rather hear Walt Whitman
or Louise Glück, anyone but me.

Away with the globe, the one I like
to spin and stop with an index
finger at those random locations
I've promised, in time, to go:

Mongolia, the Congo, the Kola
Peninsula south of the Barents Sea.

And even though I'm home now,
I will put it all away to read
each piece for consequence and
conspiracy, perhaps a bit of irony,

then spin the globe again to stop
with a finger, hopefully over you,
weeding the garden, moving

as you do so well, around the sun
without a sail to take you
in a leeward breeze of memory.

notes

Page 18. "A Short Walk on the Shimokita Peninsula": The peninsula is located at the northern tip of Honshū, Japan. I camped many times there in Yagen valley.

Page 23. "And Then the Lighting of the Lamps": The title is the last line of T.S. Eliot's "Preludes" (Part I).

Page 24. "Settling Down": The final allusion is to Knut Hamsun's novel, *Hunger*, whose main character struggles with many forms of hunger as he wanders through Kristiania, now Oslo, Norway.

Page 28. "River of Faces": Jake Mercer was a family friend and aerial gunner on an AC-130 gunship shot down over Thua Thien Province, South Vietnam, in June, 1972. His remains were discovered in October, 1993 and identified in October, 1994.

Page 33. "A Minor Ode to Poetry": With eventual thanks to Robert Burns, whose line "O my Luve is like a red, red rose" is still used by teachers to explain simile to their young students.

Page 37. "Autopsis": From the Greek (*autos* - self, *opsis* - a sight). The Royal Geographical Society pressed autopsis on its 19th century explorers as a method of observation. They encouraged the explorers to record everything they saw, regardless of its apparent triviality.

Page 52. "Before a Cold Front can Emerge": It's possible, in 2012, to have lost a father in Vietnam and a son or daughter in one of our recent wars.

acknowledgements

I'm extremely grateful to the editors of the following publications and journals, where several of these poems first appeared:

Anon Poetry Magazine (UK): "Winter Rye"

Hobble Creek Review: "Helsinki" and "Watermelon"

Linden Avenue Literary Journal: "Settling Down" and "To the Twenty-Something Girl Who Winked"

Red River Review: "Around the Sun Without a Sail" and "Poets of a Dead Language"

Storyteller: "River of Faces"

Tuck Magazine: "Halfway Point" and "Geography"

Poet's Post Volume IV Anthology: "And Then the Lighting of the Lamps," "The Barren Bits," "Burning Matches" and "Fourth of July"

I owe so much to Lonnie Hodge, my college professor and poetry mentor, who first suggested I submit poems for publication. I also wish to thank Clovita Rice, who published my first poem in the Arkansas quarterly, *Voices International.*

I must also mention my cousin, Barry DeKemper, whose cryptic marginalia in a poetry book, years ago, made me pause and wonder.

about the author

Richard Fenwick is a poet and Russian translator who works with Holocaust survivors from Belarus, Ukraine, and Russia, translating their histories for publication. His poems have been published in numerous quarterlies and journals. This is his first full collection of poetry.